My Family Tree Book

By Catherine Bruzzone

Illustrated by Caroline Jayne Church

b small publishing

www.bsmall.co.uk

A family tree

Your family tree is the map of your family. It shows how you are related, or joined, to the other people in your family – just like the branches and twigs are joined to the trunk of a tree.

The picture on page 3 shows a simple family tree.

Can you see the lines joining you to your sister and brother, mother and father and to your grandparents? These lines show how you are **related**. These people are your **relations**.

This might not look like *your* family. Perhaps you have more brothers or sisters? And you may have aunts and uncles and lots of cousins. Family trees can show all these people. They can also give you many other fascinating facts, like when your mother was born, how many brothers and sisters your grandmother has, how old your grandfather was when he died.

You will be able to draw your own family tree at the end of this book. But before you do, discover as much as you can about your family on the next pages.

You may find much more information or photos than you have room for on these pages. Clip extra paper on to the pages, or make a special envelope out of the back cover.

You could make a separate book with the extra pages. Punch holes in the edges and thread through pieces of wool to hold them together.

Cut photos to fit the spaces provided

Cut a triangle from card and glue or tape to the back cover

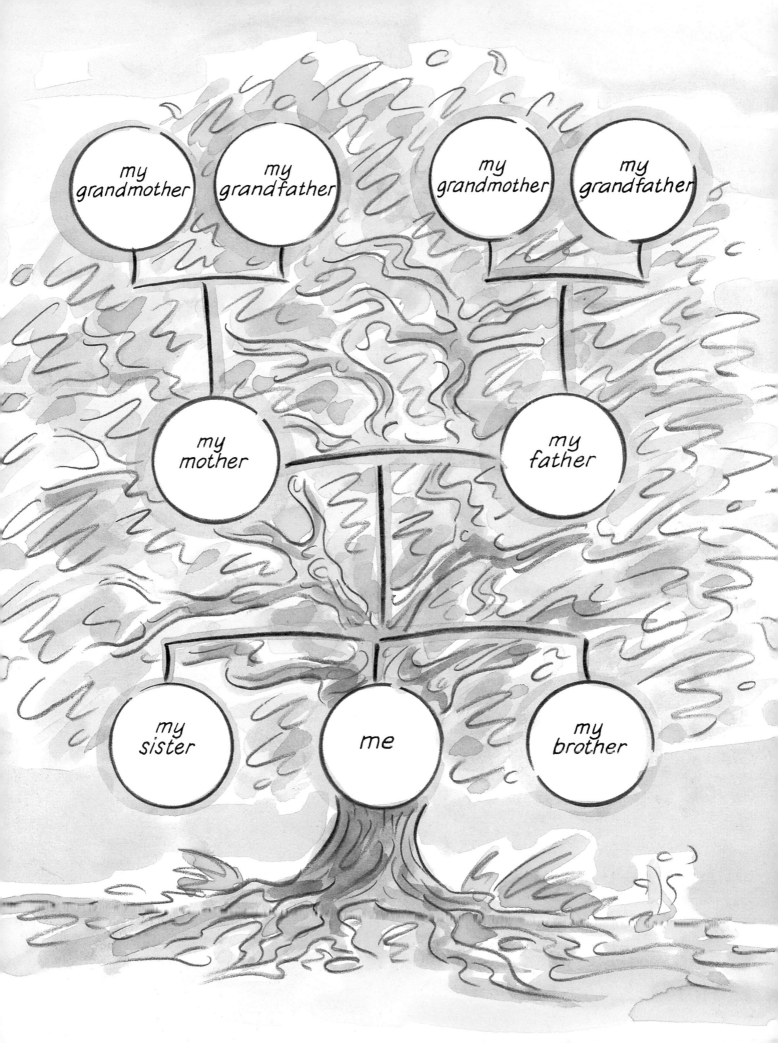

All about me

Date I was born

Mother's name

Time I was born

Father's name

Ask if you can see your birth certificate. Did someone keep a record when you were a baby?

Where I was born

Names of brothers

Weight when I was born

Names of sisters

Length when I was born

Name of person who looks after me

STICK IN PHOTOGRAPH

STICK IN PHOTOGRAPH

me as a baby

me, age ....

My name is

Other people who live with me

Languages I can speak

Where I live now

Names of schools or playgroups

Telephone number

Fill this space with more about yourself or draw a self-portrait

My mother

Number of brothers ☐
Number of sisters ☐

Date she was born

Names of brothers

_____

Where she was born

Try asking your grandparents for some of these answers. For example, they might remember what time your mother was born.

Names of sisters

_____

Time she was born

Names of schools

_____

Surname when she was born

_____

_____

STICK IN
PHOTOGRAPH

STICK IN
PHOTOGRAPH

mummy, age ....

mummy, age ....

Her name is

Certificates

Colour of hair _____

Colour of eyes _____

Favourite colour _____

Jobs

Favourite food _____

_____

Her age when I was born

_____

Draw your mother here

7

My father

Date he was born

_____

Where he was born

_____

Time he was born

_____

Number of sisters ☐
Number of brothers ☐

Names of sisters

_____

Names of brothers

_____

Names of schools

_____

_____

Try asking your grandparents for some of these answers. For example, they might remember what time your father was born.

STICK IN
PHOTOGRAPH

daddy, age ....

STICK IN
PHOTOGRAPH

daddy, age ....

His name is

Certificates

_____

Jobs

_____

His age when I was born

_____

Colour of eyes _____

Colour of hair _____

Anything else about him?

Fill this space with more about your father, or draw a picture of him

My sisters and brothers

Number of sisters ☐
Number of brothers ☐

My oldest sister or brother's name is

_____

Date she or he was born

_____

Where she or he was born

_____

My next oldest sister or brother's name is

_____

Date she or he was born

_____

Where she or he was born

_____

My next oldest sister or brother's name is

_____

Date she or he was born

_____

Where she or he was born

_____

If you have more than 3 sisters and brothers, write their details on a piece of paper and clip it to this page. You can also give details of half-sisters and brothers or stepsisters and brothers.

If you want, say how they are related to you : "Rose is my half-sister. She and I have the same father."

"Robert is my stepbrother. He is John's son. John lives with my mother."

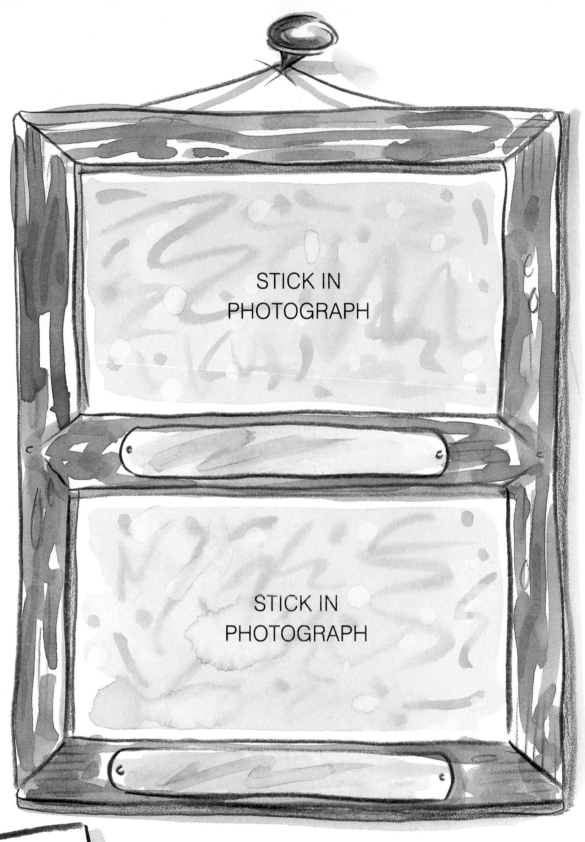

STICK IN
PHOTOGRAPH

STICK IN
PHOTOGRAPH

Who is in each photo?
How old are they?
Where were the photos taken?
When were they taken?

My aunts and uncles

These are my **mother's** sisters and brothers.

My oldest aunt or uncle's name is

_____

Date she or he was born

_____

Where she or he was born

_____

Where she or he lives now

_____

Person she or he lives with

_____

Names of children

My next oldest aunt or uncle's name is

_____

Date she or he was born

_____

Where she or he was born

_____

Where she or he lives now

_____

Person she or he lives with

_____

Names of children

Your aunts' or uncles' children are **cousins**. You can fill in more details about them on pages 16 and 17.

My next oldest aunt or uncle's name is

_____

Person she or he lives with

_____

Date she or he was born

_____

Names of children

Where she or he was born

_____

_____

Where she or he lives now

_____

If your mother has more than 3 sisters and brothers, write their details on a piece of paper and clip it here. Can you find a photo of your mother and her brothers and sisters as children?

STICK IN
PHOTOGRAPH

STICK IN
PHOTOGRAPH

Write the names of the people in each photo. Where were the photos taken? When were they taken? Do you have a photo of the same people now?

_____

_____

_____

_____

13

My aunts and uncles

These are my **father's** sisters and brothers.

My oldest aunt or uncle's name is

_____

Date she or he was born

_____

Where she or he was born

_____

Where she or he lives now

_____

Person she or he lives with

_____

Names of children

My next oldest aunt or uncle's name is

_____

Date she or he was born

_____

Where she or he was born

_____

Where she or he lives now

_____

Person she or he lives with

_____

Names of children

Do you have any **cousins**? These are your aunts' and uncles' children. Fill in their details on pages 16 and 17.

_____

My next oldest aunt or uncle's name is

_____

Date she or he was born

_____

Where she or he was born

_____

Where she or he lives now

_____

Person she or he lives with

_____

Names of children

See if you can find a photo of your father and his brothers and sisters as children.

STICK IN PHOTOGRAPH

STICK IN PHOTOGRAPH

Write the names of the people in each photo. Where and when were the photos taken? Do you have a picture of some of the people now?

_____

_____

_____

_____

My cousins –
on my mother's side

If your parents come from a large family, you may have lots of cousins! Start on your mother's side. First put her oldest brother or sister's name and then fill in the details for each cousin.

Their parents' names

Their parents' names

_____

Name of oldest son or daughter

Name of oldest son or daughter

_____

Date and place he or she was born

Date and place he or she was born

_____

Name of next oldest son or daughter

Name of next oldest son or daughter

_____

Date and place he or she was born

Date and place he or she was born

_____

My cousins – on my father's side

Paste a photo of your cousins on a sheet of paper. Under it, write their names and how old they are.

Their parents' names

Name of oldest son or daughter

Date and place he or she was born

Name of next oldest son or daughter

Date and place he or she was born

Their parents' names

Name of oldest son or daughter

Date and place he or she was born

Name of next oldest son or daughter

Date and place he or she was born

If you don't have a photo of your cousins, draw a picture of them. Which of your cousins is the tallest and which is the smallest?

My grandmother – my mother's mother

Her name is

_____

Name I call her

_____

Surname when she was born

_____

Date she was born

_____

Where she was born

_____

Date and place she was married

If your grand-parents are no longer alive, you may need to do some detective work to fill in these pages. Can your mother and father help? Or your aunts and uncles?

Names of sisters

_____

Names of brothers

_____

Name of school

_____

Jobs

_____

Age when my mother was born

_____

Something she remembers from the past

STICK IN
PHOTOGRAPH

my grandmother, age ....

18

My grandfather – my mother's father

His name is
_____

Name I call him
_____

Date he was born
_____

Where he was born
_____

Names of sisters
_____

Names of brothers
_____

Name of school
_____

Jobs
_____

Age when my mother was born
_____

Something he remembers from the past
_____

STICK IN
PHOTOGRAPH

my grandfather, age ....

Ask about the things that were different when your grandparents were young. What style of clothes did they wear? What games did they play? Can they remember something important in the news? Why not make a book or a cassette recording of their memories?

My grandmother – my father's mother

Her name is
_____

Name I call her
_____

Surname when she was born
_____

Date she was born
_____

Where she was born
_____

Date and place she was married

Names of sisters
_____

Names of brothers
_____

Name of school
_____

Jobs
_____

Age when my father was born
_____

Something she remembers from the past

STICK IN
PHOTOGRAPH

my grandmother, age ....

Look at the notes on pages 18 and 19

My grandfather – my father's father

His name is

_____

Name I call him

_____

Date he was born

_____

Where he was born

_____

Names of sisters

_____

Names of brothers

_____

Name of school

_____

Jobs

_____

Age when my father was born

_____

Something he remembers from
the past

STICK IN
PHOTOGRAPH

my grandfather, age ....

Can someone show you your grandparents' marriage certificate? It will tell you when and where they were married.

My own family tree

Fill in your own family tree here.

To start with, do a simple one – just your sisters and brothers, your parents and your grandparents. For your brothers and sisters, put the eldest on your left and the younger ones on your right. (Look at the tree on page 3 as a guide.)

If you want, ask someone to help you make a larger tree. This could show your aunts and uncles, your cousins, and perhaps your grandparents' brothers and sisters – or even your great-grandparents! You could add more details to your tree, like:

b. = born
m. = married
d. = died

Granny Black
b. 1 June 1923
Swansea

Discovering more about your family

Did your parents or grandparents keep their school reports? They will be very interesting – and may be funny too!

Do your parents have any letters or papers to show how much they earned in their first jobs? Or perhaps old uniforms or pictures of themselves at work?

Did anyone in your family keep a diary? Perhaps of a special occasion or a family holiday?

If some of your family comes from another part of the world, trace or photocopy a map and mark the different countries.

In the local library, you might find out more about the year you were born and the years your parents or grandparents were born. What styles of clothes did people wear? What songs did they enjoy?

What new things were invented – and what wasn't yet invented? Can your teacher help you?

What about the place you or your family were born? Can you find old postcards of the past?

Ask to see tombstones, old samplers or old family books (like the Bible). These could help you discover even more about your family.

If you search the internet, you will find lots of useful websites on family history. Look for your local Family History Society and see if you can join.

Published by b small publishing ltd.
The Book Shed, 36 Leyborne Park, Kew, Richmond, Surrey, TW9 3HA, UK
www.bsmall.co.uk
Text and illustrations © b small publishing, 1991
This edition first published 2006

4 5

Printed in China by WKT Co. Ltd.

British Library Cataloguing-in-Publication Data.
A record of this book is available from the British Library.
ISBN-10: 1-905710-15-1
ISBN-13: 978-1-905710-15-7